Win at
Pocket Billiards

Win at Pocket Billiards

Bank and Kick Shots Simplified,
Explained and Illustrated

by Desmond Allen, Ph.D.

Bonus Books, Inc., Chicago

05 04 03 02 01   5 4 3 2 1

Library of Congress Control Number: 2001087435
ISBN: 1-56625-163-X

Bonus Books, Inc.
160 East Illinois Street
Chicago, Illinois 60611

Printed in the United States of America

To my dear friend and mentor, Denny Salvadore. We have spent many years and countless hours at the table, and without his influence and instruction this book could never have been written.

Table of Contents

Introduction

The purpose of this handbook is to diagram and explain various one-, two- and three-rail kick shots. It is the book I always wanted to buy but could never find. I often wondered if such shots were the highly guarded secrets of the elite. Indeed, for many decades they were just that. Like the martial arts, they were passed down from master to student with the understanding that this knowledge was not to be shared with just anyone. After all, the more people who knew these shots, the stiffer the competition would be, and thus the slimmer the pickin's. It has taken me years to learn them. The majority I have learned from others. A few I have realized for myself.

Whether you are a C- or even B-player, you will benefit from these shots. In fact, I have met A-players who did not know some of them. I have taken for granted that the reader will understand the various terms employed: running English, long rail, short rail, extended diamond, etc. For those not familiar with them, I have provided a glossary of some of the more common terms.

You will find some shots a little more difficult than others. But it is good to know and master them all. Some shots may need adjustment to accommodate individual style and equipment. One player's stroke will differ from another's, thereby affecting the outcome of a given shot. The condition of the cloth, the condition of the rails, a different tip, a different shaft, even the temperature and humidity will affect a shot. Therefore, these shots may need a little modification to fit your particular situation. However, the basic premise of each will hold true.

If studied and mastered, these shots will bring you great pleasure and certainly you will win more games. They will get you out of seemingly impossible hooks. You will pocket and kick balls you never imagined possible. Your pool buddies will be amazed. They will ask, "How did you do that?" But these are not trick shots. They are not contrived shots "tailor-made" for balls in a particular, unrealistic situation. These are shot principles adaptable to real game circumstances. Obviously, not every shot will work in every situation. In fact, in most situations none of the shots are applicable. But the time will come for each, when you'll be glad you know it.

Desmond Allen, Ph.D.
March 2001

Part One

The Three-Rail Kicking System

Not long ago, I was playing 9-ball with a fellow I had never met before. Like many players, he had a good eye for pocketing balls, but obviously lacked any knowledge of the various paths that circle the table. Any time he fired a shot that rounded a second or third rail, it was anybody's guess (in his mind) as to where the cue ball might actually end up.

I had just sunk the 5-ball, leaving the cue ball in the middle of the table. The 6-ball, 7-ball and 9-ball were clustered in the side pocket. Although I had an easy shot on the 6-ball, as far as he could see, I had no way to get shape on the 7-ball.

"Looks like I'll get another shot," he said.

I remained silent, but thought to myself, "I don't think so!" Little did he know, I had planned this position on the 6-ball back when I came to the table at the 4-ball. I knew that once I cleared the 4- and 5-ball out of the way there was an excellent path for the cue ball to go three rails off the 6-ball to get great position on the 7-ball (*Figure 1*).

"Boy, you got lucky there!" he said.

He had a cocky attitude, so I just agreed with him and finished the rack. He left that day never realizing just how routine the shot really was.

The knowledge for this shot, and many more like it, is based upon the three-rail kicking system, simply called "the System" by many players. As far as bank and kicking methods go, this is the Grand-Daddy of them all. And it would be inappropriate to start this manual with anything else.

Of course, no system is perfect. It would be foolish to expect one to be. There are too many variables in both the equipment and the players. But there are certain fundamentals that to some degree can be relied upon. It is upon these principles that this and other systems are built.

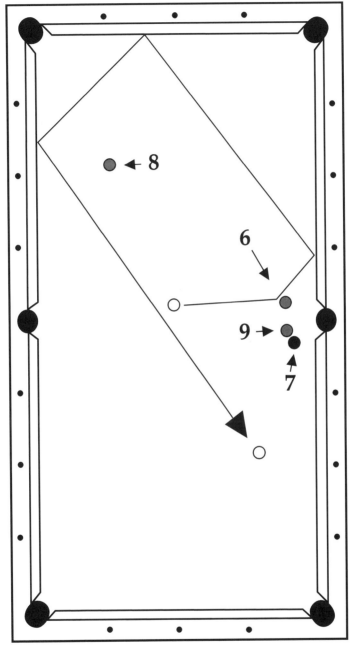

Figure 1

THE SYSTEM

The next few pages are technical, but critical. I suggest that you study them at the pool table with cue in hand. Practice each lesson as you read it.

In the game of carom billiards, the System is used to make a billiard on a ball after the cue ball has rounded the table, contacting three rails. In pocket billiards (generally referred to as pool), we take the shot a step further, using it to kick balls along the forth rail as well. Sometimes we even use this shot to pocket a ball.

It is a fantastic shot to watch. No matter how many times you see it, it is still amazing. The cue ball circles the table to kick a ball along the fourth rail just as planned. It is even more fun to execute. You simply have to admire the shot and its relative simplicity.

THE COUNT

In order to use the System, you must first understand its count. By count, I am referring to the methods for numbering both the position and the path of the cue ball. The first count signifies the position of the cue ball. Or more precisely, the starting point of the path that will take the cue ball to a desired point of the third rail. The second count designates the expected contact points along the first and third rails.

This creates an interesting scenario that confuses many. But to understand the System, you must learn to count the diamonds using both methods. There are two counts along the third rail. Cue ball position count, P#, and contact point count, D# (*Figure 2*). This means, for example, that while the side pocket is position three (P3) for cue ball position count, at the same time, it is dia-

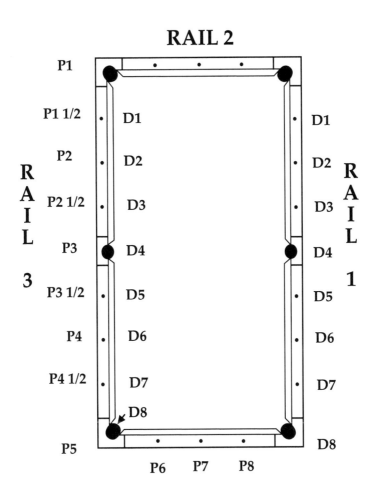

Figure 2

mond four (D4) as far as the contact point of the cue ball along the third rail is concerned. Once you understand these principles you are on your way to seeing the simplicity of the System.

Position Count

Using the first numbering method to distinguish the cue ball position number (P#), stand at the corner of the table from which the cue ball will be shot (i.e., stand at P5 in *Figure 2*) and look up the long rail. The diamonds along that rail denote positions in half increments. The first position (P1), is an imaginary diamond in the back of the corner pocket at the other end of the rail. Coming back down the rail, the first diamond is P1½. The second diamond is P2, the third is P2½, the fourth is P3, the fifth is P3½, the sixth is P4, the seventh is P4½, the eighth is P5, where you are standing. The diamonds along the foot rail denote positions in full increments. They're P6, P7 and P8.

Diamond Count

The second numbering method uses the diamonds to mark the path of the cue ball on its way around the table. Here the diamonds are simply counted per diamond as they come down each rail (*Figure 2*). Along the long rails the first diamonds are D1; the second diamonds are D2; the third, D3; the fourth, D4 (the side pockets); the fifth, D5; the sixth, D6; the seventh, D7; the eighth, D8.

THE FORMULA FOR THE SYSTEM

A ball stroked with running English toward the first rail will contact those points along the first and third rails that total the position number from which the cue ball begins its journey. The formula is: Position # = Rail 1 # + Rail 3 #, or P# = D# along rail one + D# along rail two. In simple English this means the cue ball position equals the contact point on rail one plus the contact point on rail three. Or we can state it backwards. The total count of the contact points along rails one and three equals the starting position of the cue ball (*Figure 3*).

For example, a ball coming out of position five with running English, going to the first diamond on the first rail will go to the fourth diamond on the third rail. One plus four equals five. If the ball is hit to diamond two from the same position, it will go to diamond three on the third rail. Hit to diamond three and it will go to diamond two on the third rail. Hit to diamond four and it will go to diamond one on the third rail. Hit to diamond five and it will go to diamond zero, which is the corner pocket. The same holds true for a ball coming out of any other position. The sum of the contact points along the first and third rail will equal the position of the cue ball (*Figure 3*).

RAIL 2

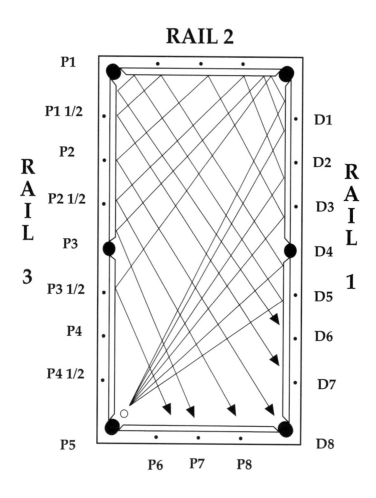

Figure 3

THE FORMULA TO THE CORNER POCKET

The final piece of the puzzle, which is very useful for our purposes in pocket billiards, is this: a ball stroked with running English, medium speed, coming off the second diamond along the third rail goes to the corner pocket. Therefore, P# - 2 = PA; that is, the position of the cue ball minus two, equals the point of aim on the first rail. So that, from out of the corner pocket, position five, with running English and a medium stroke through the third diamond on the first rail, the cue ball goes from the second diamond on the third rail to the corner pocket. A cue ball anywhere along the path from position five, to the third diamond on the first rail is said to be in P5 (*Figure 3*).

Now here is where application of the art is necessary. This is what makes it difficult for some to apply the System with success. The System is designed to kick along the third rail. It is based on a mathematical formula of angles and it works with great percussion on any table (P# = R1 + R3). That is the constant. However, where the ball goes on the return track from the third rail to the fourth rail is particular to each table. This will depend on all the variables you can imagine: the type of balls, the balance of the balls, the tip, the stroke and the condition the table, to name a few. For example, new cloth will play longer than worn cloth. The more worn and soiled the cloth becomes, the shorter it will play. Even the humidity on a given day can affect the cue ball's position on the return track. But here is the good news: once you know how a certain table plays, it will be consistent. It only takes a few practice shots to find out how a table is playing the return track.

It has been my experience that many, if not most, pocket billiards tables play this shot a little short. That is, on most tables, with my stroke I play the shot about one-half diamond longer. Therefore, when ideally I should be aiming at the third diamond on the first rail, I aim at diamond 2½. The bottom line is, know how the equipment responds. Before playing on a new table, or before a match, test it. Know what to expect on a given table on a given day.

KICKING OFF THE THIRD RAIL

One final piece of information before we look at a few examples. When using the System to kick balls that are just off the third rail, adjustments are made roughly in parallel. The second diamond on the third rail goes to the corner pocket. Likewise, the first diamond off the third rail goes to diamond seven on the long fourth rail. And the third diamond on the third rail goes to the first diamond on the short fourth rail (*Figure 3*).

THE FORMULA TO KICK ALONG THE FOURTH RAIL

With these basic concepts understood there are numerous applications available. Let's suppose that from position five you need to kick a half diamond up the long fourth rail (*Figure 4*). Simply add another half diamond to the point of aim on the first rail, P5 - 2 = D3 (to get to the corner pocket), then add a half diamond to come up the rail. The total is D3½. Aim at diamond 3½.

Suppose you need to kick one diamond down the short fourth rail. Subtract one diamond from the point of aim on the first rail, P5 - 2 = D3 (to get to the corner pocket), - 1 = D2. Aim at diamond two on the first rail (*Figure 5*).

To get to the corner pocket from position four, the point of aim with running English is the second diamond on the first rail (P4 - 2 = D2), (*Figure 6*).

If the cue ball is in position 5½, the point of aim for the corner pocket is D3½ on the first rail (P5½ - 2 = D3½), (*Figure 7*).

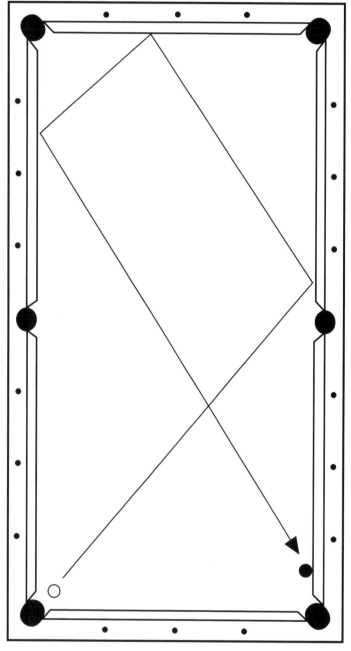

Figure 4

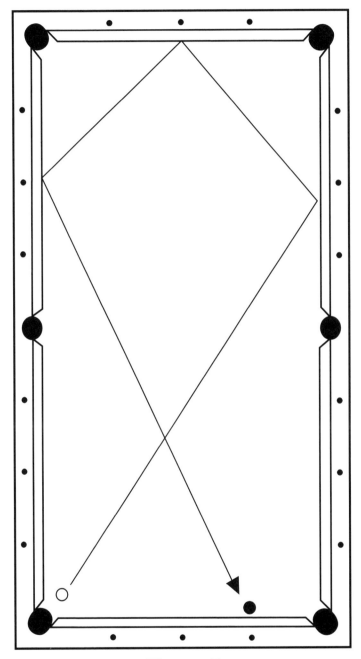

Figure 5

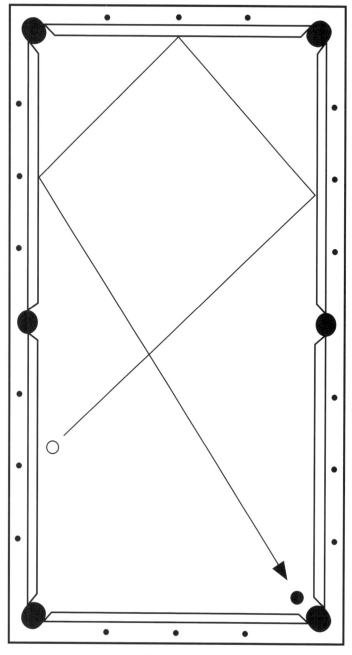

Figure 6

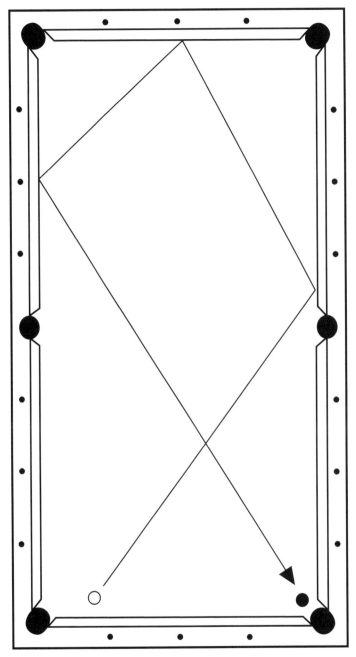

Figure 7

HOOKED IN 14.1

Now let's apply this system to a situation (*Figure 8*). You are playing 14.1 continuous and your opponent has played safe, leaving you hooked behind the cluster. You are expecting to play safe yourself or maybe even take a deliberate foul. But, there are a couple of balls kissing along the long rail. You see that the cue ball is in the path of position 4½. Therefore, the point of aim to get to the corner pocket is D2½ on the first rail (that is, barring adjustments for the equipment). But you need to kick the kissing balls one-half diamond up the long fourth rail. Adjust by adding a half diamond to your point of aim. Aim at D3 on the first rail.

At first you may think this is a risky shot to attempt in 14.1 continuous. If you miss, your opponent might run 30 or 40 balls on you. But this shot is all but wire. I just went to the table and made it eight times in a row before missing. On the ninth attempt I hit the balls too softly and the called ball failed to reach the pocket. Then I made it another five times before quitting. Furthermore, I got good position on the next shot at the bottom of the rack (a break ball), on almost every attempt.

After this little research project, I was feeling quite confident about this shot. So I urged the first person who walked in the door to come over and try it. "I'll tell you were to hit it," I said. I told her what to do, and the cue ball rounded the table and headed straight for the kissing balls. Coming down the return track it started losing speed. The last eighteen inches or so I wondered if it would make it to the object ball. Then, when it finally made contact, I wondered if it had enough energy to sink the ball. You should have seen the grin on her face as the called ball crept closer and closer to the pocket, like a bather afraid of the cold water, before finally diving in. It's an amazing shot!

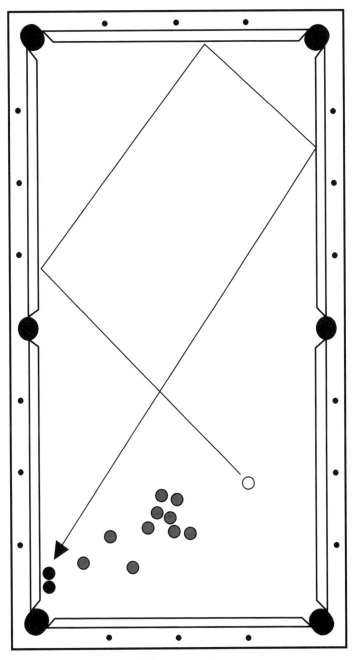

Figure 8

HOOKED IN 9-BALL

Here is another situation. You are playing 9-ball and your opponent has left you hooked (*Figure 9*). The 3-ball, your next shot, is a few inches off the long rail. You see that the cue ball is in position four. The 3-ball is in the path of D2½ on the third rail, and about D½ along the short fourth rail. Remember the formula, P4 - 2 = D2 (to the pocket) - ½ = D1½. Consequently you aim at D1½, on the first rail to kick the 3-ball which is just off the third rail, thereby avoiding a foul and ball in hand for your opponent.

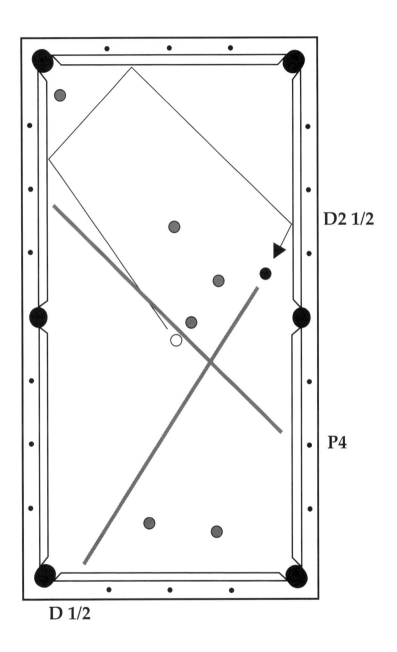

D2 1/2

P4

D 1/2

Figure 9

SOME POSITION SHOTS ON THE 8-BALL

This system is also very accurate for determining and achieving cue ball position. For example, you are shooting your last solid and need to get position on the 8-ball (*Figure 10*). The problem is that you are shooting the object ball into the side pocket and the 8-ball is on the center diamond along the foot rail. You know you have to go three rails to get there, but where will the cue ball go? Will you have position? Will you scratch?

Using the System, these questions can be answered even before you shoot. By cheating the pocket you can alter, to some degree, the tangent line of the cue ball off the solid. Therefore, you can select the area of the first rail that you want to contact in order to control the final position of the cue ball. This shot can be made with a rather high degree of accuracy once you understand the paths. In our example, the tangent line of the cue ball off the object ball is coming out of P5½ and headed to diamond 2½ on the first rail. This should take the cue ball about one diamond down the short fourth rail. You'll avoid the foul and get great position on the 8-ball.

P5 1/2

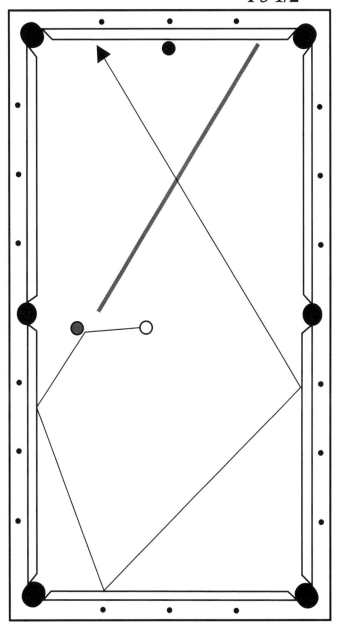

Figure 10

Position Example 1

Another example of how the knowledge of this system can help you achieve the position you need is seen in *Figure 11*. You have an easy shot on your last stripe, but how are you going to get shape on the 8-ball? The answer: use a little right English and the cue ball will come off the rail near position 4½ and head toward diamond two on the opposite long rail. P4½ minus D2 equals D2½. The cue ball should come to rest somewhere near D2½, leaving you a nice shot on the 8-ball. In this situation you don't even have to reach the fourth rail to get the desired position. This makes the shot even more appealing in that it affords a high margin for error.

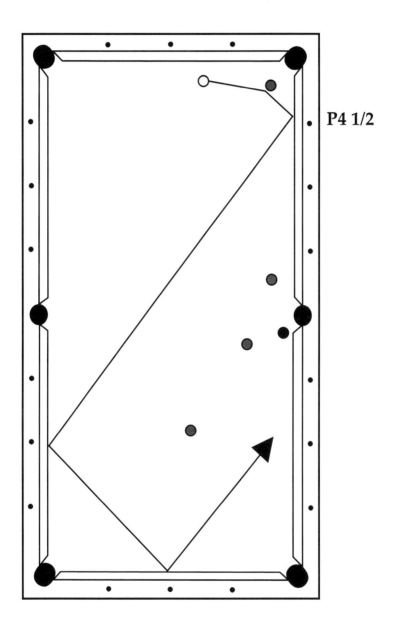

P4 1/2

Figure 11

Position Example 2

Here, too, you need position on the 8-ball. You have all but a straight-in shot on your last solid, but the 8-ball is along the long rail, blocked by the stripes. Using the System, you see that if you were to follow the object ball and contact the first rail at about diamond three, you would be on track P5½ which will take you to diamond 2½ on the third rail. There, you'll have perfect position of the 8-ball (*Figure 12*).

P5 1/2

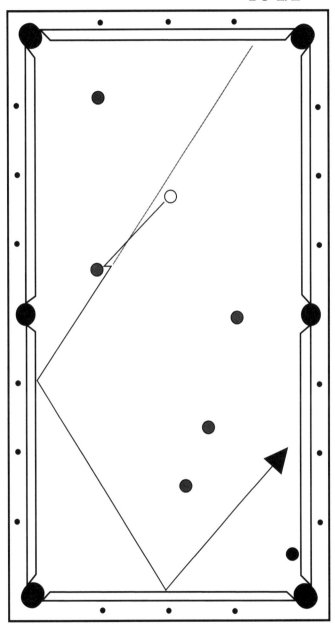

Figure 12

SEE THE DANGER ZONES

By using the System, you will also learn to see the danger zones. By danger zone I mean those shots that have a good chance of scratching, such as illustrated in *Figure 13*. You have an easy shot on the 8-ball and need to go up to the end of the table for position on the 9-ball. That seems easy enough, just give it a slow-medium stroke with a little running English and it will easily take you up the table. But if you get careless with this easy shot, there is danger lurking at the other end of the table.

The tangent line of the cue ball will put it on the path from P6 on the foot rail to D6 on the first rail. Position six, minus the diamond six on the first rail leaves diamond zero on the third rail, which just happens to be the corner pocket. Careful observation reveals this is a scratch shot. Avoid it simply by adding a little low left English to the shot. This will lengthen the tangent line and bring the contact point on the first rail up to diamond five. Diamond five will then take you to diamond one on the third rail.

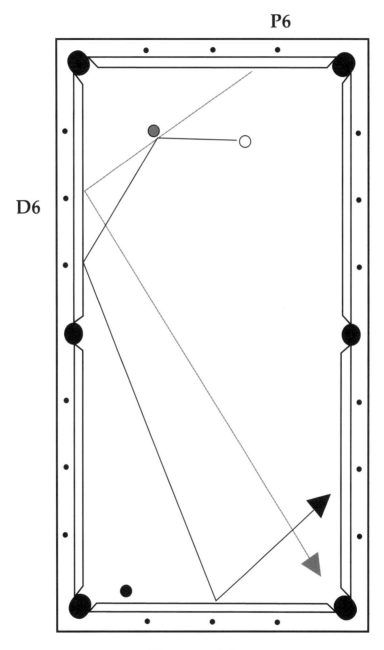

Figure 13

ALTERNATE METHODS

There are other methods for applying the System without actually using the formula. On any given table, once you know the path from the corner pocket (P5) to the first rail that leads to the other corner pocket along the fourth rail, you can apply one of two alternative methods. The first is to make adjustments in parallel. For cue ball positions along the foot rail, adjust in parallels to the original reference path. For cue ball positions up the long rail, determine the parallel path and then divide the distance between the two in half. This determines the point of aim to get to the pocket (*Figure 14*). From here, make other adjustments for fourth rail kicks by adding and subtracting the distance per diamond as noted above.

The second method also relies upon knowing the path that takes you from corner pocket to corner pocket. Once it is identified, extend that path about five feet beyond the rail and mark a reference or vanishing point. Generally it will be a spot on another table or the wall. Use this vanishing point as a point of aim from nearly anywhere on the table and it will take you to the corner pocket.

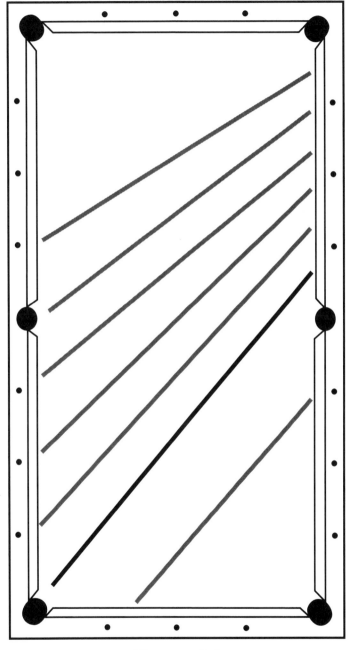

Figure 14

Part Two

Two-Rail
Kick Shots

SHORT RAIL FIRST AND TURN
BACK TOWARD CORNER POCKET

This is a shot my old friend Denny Salvadore showed me many years ago. Denny is the kind of guy you don't want to bet against. He seems to live a charmed life. If I could buy stock in him, I would. A star athlete, an excellent poker player and a hustler from the word go, he never ceases to amaze me. Fifteen years ago while playing drop-in basketball at a local gym, I watched him make three shots in a row from half court to win a bet. He was 39 years old at the time. Do yourself a favor: if ever you should meet him, don't make any wagers.

From off the first diamond on the long rail you can turn the cue ball back to the corner pocket. In *Figure 15*, you need to kick the 8-ball, but you are hooked. With the butt of the cue slightly elevated, use extreme outside English about three o'clock (adjust for equipment and stroke). Aim a smooth medium-hard stroke just off the last diamond on the short rail. The cue ball will go two rails and turn back toward the corner pocket. It almost looks magical.

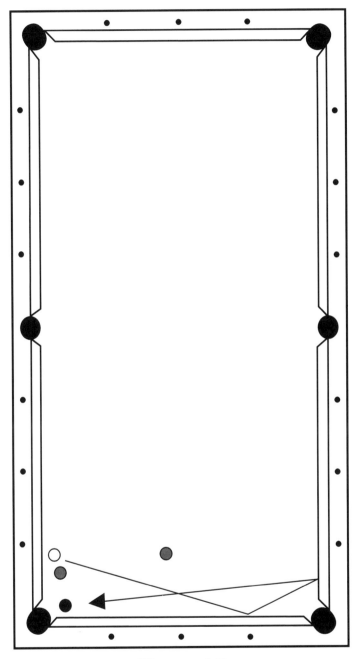

Figure 15

LONG RAIL FIRST AND TURN BACK TOWARD SIDE POCKET

This shot is basically the same as the last, but along the long rail (*Figure 16*). Like the last shot, it too seems almost magical. There is a path from the third diamond on the foot rail to the last diamond on the long rail that leads back to the side pocket. With the butt of the cue slightly elevated, use extreme outside English about three o'clock (adjust for equipment and stroke). Again, a smooth medium-hard stroke and the cue ball will turn back toward the side pocket on the first rail. Adjusting in parallel, this path actually extends all the way to the next set of diamonds (i.e., D2 on the foot rail to D6 on the long rail).

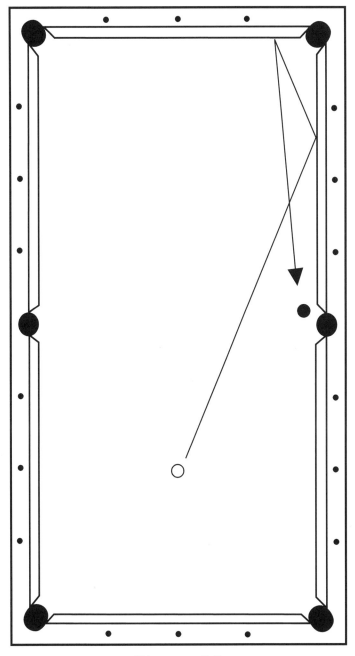

Figure 16

SHORT RAIL FIRST TO CORNER POCKET (357)

As a memory tool, I call this shot the "357." I chose this name because the diamonds at the end of the three paths total three, five and seven. That is, the first path is between D2 on the long rail and D1 on the short rail. The total is three. The second path is between D3 on the long rail and D2 on the short rail. The total is five. The third path is between D4 on the long rail and D3 on the short rail. The total is seven, thus "357."

Using one tip of inside English with a slow to medium stroke there is a path coming out of diamond four, the near side pocket, to the third diamond on the top rail which leads to the near corner pocket (*Figure 17*). Adjustments are made in parallel until you are within the path that extends from diamond three on the long rail to diamond two on the short rail (or path 3). Inside this path, adjustments are made by determining the ball's parallel path to the short rail, and then dividing the distance to path D3-D2 in half to find the point of aim.

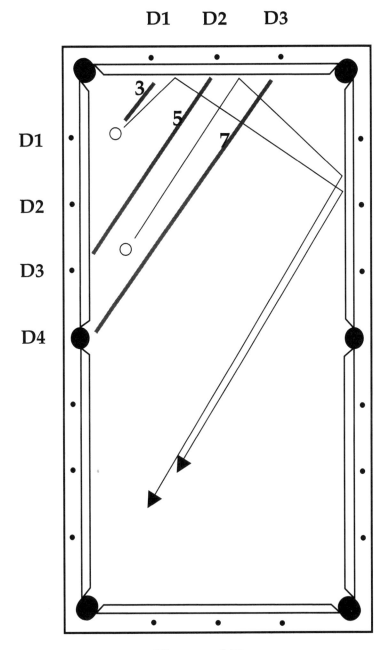

Figure 17

LONG RAIL FIRST TO CORNER POCKET (22 LONG)

The line of reference for this two-rail kick shot to the corner pocket is a path from diamond two on the short rail to roughly the point of the extended diamond two on the long rail. As you might guess, as a memory tool for this shot I call it the "22 Long," from diamond two, to diamond two on the long rail.

Stroke the cue ball with a medium stroke using center ball. Here too, adjustments are made in parallel. However, as the position of the cue ball moves nearer to the rail, further adjustments must be made to allow for the greater amount of natural English imparted by the steeper angle of contact with the rail. Therefore, aim an inch or so further down the rail (*Figure 18*). This shot may sound easier than it is. For accuracy it must be hit center ball, unfortunately this is a problem for most of us.

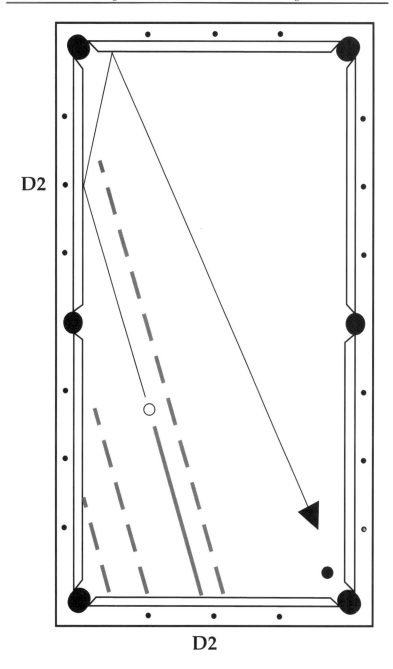

D2

D2

Figure 18

Part Three

One-Rail
Kick Shots

There are several systems for figuring one-rail kick and bank shots. Although some of these systems accomplish the same thing, I advise that you learn them all and use the one that best fits the situation in which you find yourself when the need arises.

KNIGHT KICK TO CORNER POCKET

A favorite shot of mine is one I have called the Knight Kick, named after the Knight's moving pattern in the game of chess (1, 2 and over). The pattern of this kicking system is to count down 2½ diamonds along the rail to determine the parallel point on the opposite rail, which is the point of aim (*Figure 19*). From out of the fifth diamond along the near long rail, a ball stroked center ball to the extended point of D2½ on the opposite rail will go to the corner pocket. By starting point, I am speaking of the diamond (not the extended point) on the near rail that marks the beginning of the path that leads to the pocket. A ball anywhere along this path, that is, from out of the diamond to the point of aim 2½ diamonds down, will go the corner pocket.

Now, bring the starting point to the sixth diamond and aim 2½ diamonds down the opposite rail with one-half tip of inside English and you'll get to the corner pocket as well. Bring the starting point to the seventh diamond and aim at 2½ diamonds down the opposite rail with one tip of inside English and you go to the pocket. Bring the starting point to the eighth diamond (the corner pocket). Using extreme English, aim 2½ diamonds down the opposite rail and you'll go to the pocket.

It's an easy system to remember. The further the starting point is from the fifth diamond, simply add a little more English. The English is adjusted in increments of roughly one-half tip per diamond. Take note, however, this shot requires a smooth stroke in order to apply the necessary spin on the cue ball. As with other shots, adjustments can be made to kick balls that are near, but not actually on the path to the pocket.

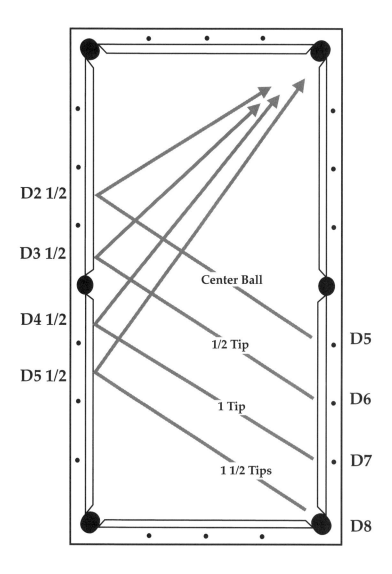

Figure 19

KNIGHT KICK TO SIDE RAIL

If you continue the Knight Kick theory to the other side of the table, you will see a very useful pattern develop. From out of the fourth diamond (the side pocket), aiming 2½ diamonds down the opposite rail, a slow stroke using center ball leads to the extended point of the third diamond on the short rail. Use one-half tip of inside English and it goes to the second diamond. One tip of English goes to the first diamond (*Figure 20*).

Now bring the starting point to the third diamond. Aim 2½ diamonds down the opposite rail with center ball and it goes to the extended point of the first diamond on the short rail. Use one-half tip of English and it goes to the ½ diamond. One tip of English goes to the ¼ diamond and then it comes back to the third diamond on the long rail, your starting point.

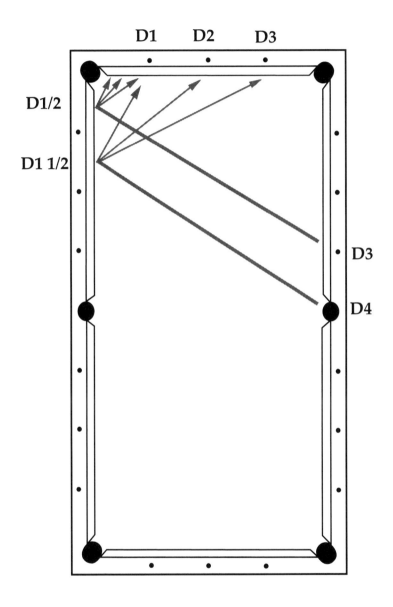

Figure 20

CENTER LINE KICK

This system is a great tool for kicking to both the side and corner pockets. It is easily mastered and very versatile.

Working length-ways on the table, from anywhere along the center line a slow to medium stroke with about a tip and a half of inside English will kick to the side pocket (*Figure 21a*). For balls off center line, simply adjust the point of aim by half parallels. As shown in *Figure 22*, this works from both right and left of center line.

To kick along the width of the table simply divide the table in half at the corner pockets and then identify the center line. This will be either the head string or the foot spot depending upon the side of the table you are working. With a stroke similar to the one described above, only slightly softer, you are able to kick to either the side of the corner pocket (*Figure 21b*). I believe the softer stroke is necessary because the cue ball position is closer to the rail in most of these shots than when kicking off the short rail.

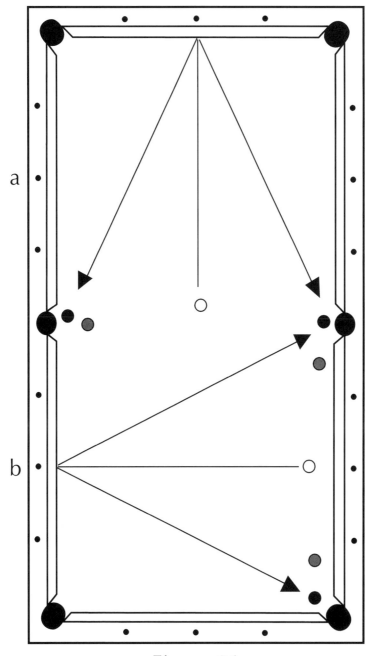

Figure 21

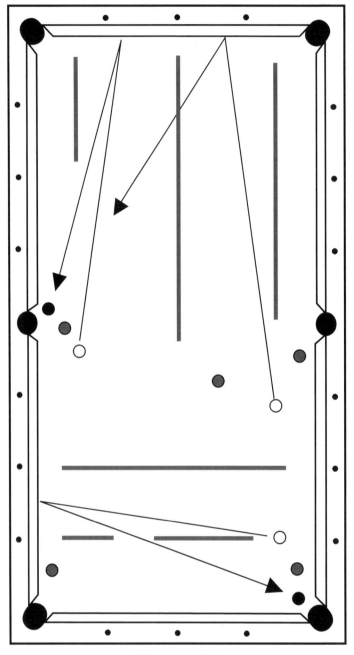

Figure 22

THE 8-2-8 KICK

It takes a little more practice to develop accuracy in this shot than in some of the others. I call it the 8-2-8 kick for the following reason. With the butt of the cue stick slightly elevated, using a medium stroke with about 1½ tips of low inside English, from out of the corner pocket (diamond eight), to the second diamond on the top rail, the cue ball will come back to the corner pocket.

What makes this shot so useful is that it adjusts in parallels. Suppose the cue ball were near the side pocket, but you needed to kick a ball in the corner pocket (*Figure* 23). Simply adjust the point of aim along the top rail in parallel. Although this is best for kicking balls into the corner pockets, it can also be used for kicking balls along the foot rail. But, accuracy is critical.

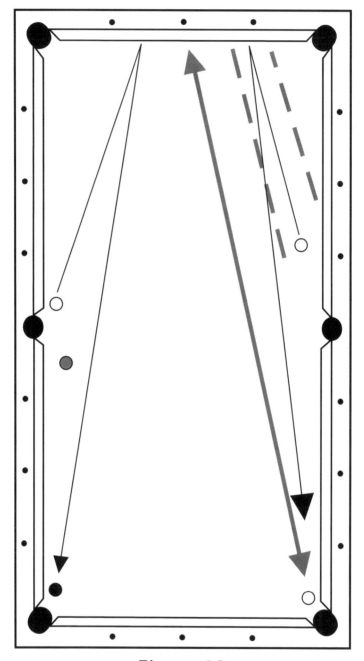

Figure 23

POSITION KICK

For this shot we refer back to the position count of the three-rail kicking system (*Figure 3*). But here the position number is going to identify the object ball rather than the cue ball. Determine the position of the object ball, then equate that number to each diamond and/or fraction thereof, along the foot rail. Determine the diamond on the foot rail from which the cue ball's path would originate. Add the total count. View the diamonds on the top rail as 10, 20 and 30. Aim the cue ball to the point on the top rail that equals the projected starting point of the path of the cue ball. There are examples provided in figures 24 and 25.

In *Figure 24*, the position of the object ball is P4½. Therefore, each diamond on the foot rail is worth 4½. The cue ball is on a path coming out of the third diamond. So the point of aim is 13½ on the top rail.

In *Figure 25* the object ball is near three. That makes each diamond along the foot rail worth three. The cue ball is on a path that originates a little past the second diamond. Since the diamonds for this particular object ball are worth three, there are two counts between each diamond. That makes the imaginary projected path of the cue ball begin out of count seven. Aim at seven on the top rail.

When using this particular system to kick, be very careful to use center ball. Even the least amount of English will affect the shot.

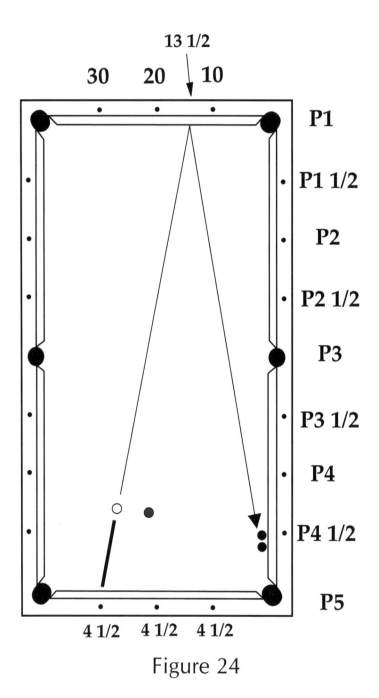

Figure 24

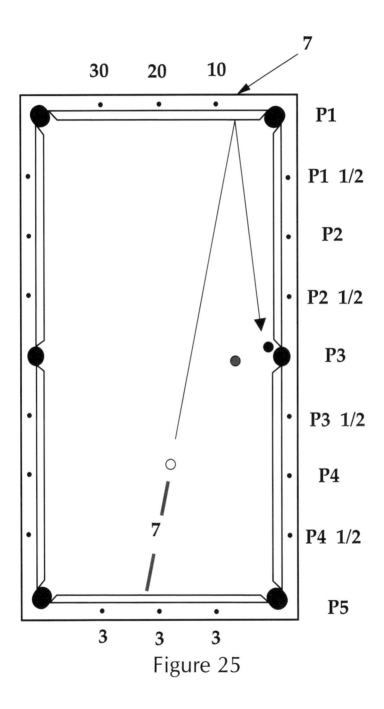

Figure 25

PERCENTAGE KICK

In order to explain this shot, let's assume the table is only half its size. That is, we are dealing with only one end of the table, from the side pockets to one set of corner pockets. By starting from any one of the pockets in the square, the target pocket is the pocket along the same long rail. In *Figure 26*, the starting point is the left side pocket. The target pocket is the left corner pocket. Various points on the opposite rail can be used to get to the target pocket. Each requires a certain amount of English. By dividing the opposite rail into fractions or percentages to determine a particular point of aim, the corresponding English can be selected with a high degree of accuracy. Study the following chart. It is not that difficult to memorize.

12½% a slow stroke with extreme inside English

25% a slow stroke with 1½ tips of inside English

37½% a slow-medium stroke with one tip of inside English

50% a slow-medium stroke hit center ball

62½% a medium stroke with one tip of outside English

75% a medium-hard stoke with extreme low outside English, butt slightly elevated

87½% a hard stroke with extreme low outside English, butt slightly elevated

This system can also be applied to shots that are not in line from pocket to pocket. Simply identify the zero and 100% marks and make adjustments accordingly.

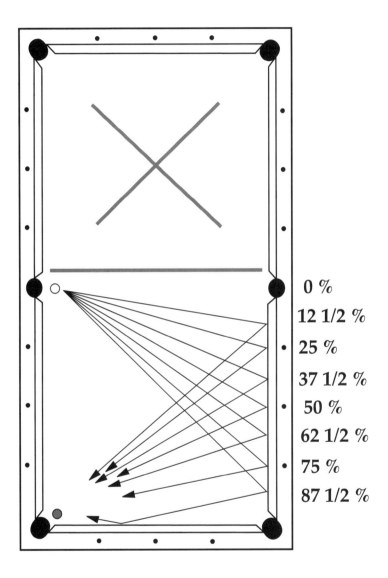

0 %
12 1/2 %
25 %
37 1/2 %
50 %
62 1/2 %
75 %
87 1/2 %

Figure 26

Let's look at the shot in action. This is a shot I made a some time ago in a local 9-ball tournament. I was hooked on the 3-ball (*Figure 27*). I could have kicked it from the long rail, but I would have had no chance of pocketing the ball. I elected to use this percent kick shot. I determined that the cue ball was on the path coming out of the side pocket heading to about 83% down the opposite rail. I hit the cue ball with a medium stroke using extreme low outside English, about 4:30. The cue ball came off the rail, curved back toward the 3-ball and kicked it into the pocket. From there I was able to run out.

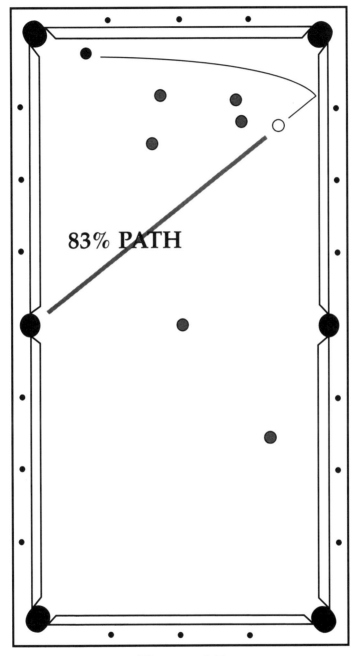

Figure 27

Figure 28 illustrates yet another example of the percentage shot. Here the cue ball is on the path of percentage 25. Use a slow stroke with about 1½ tips of English.

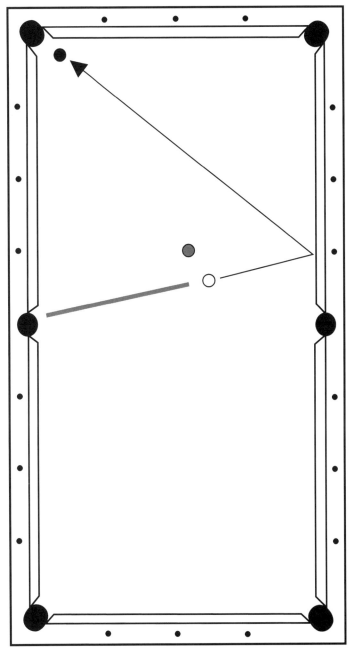

Figure 28

GEOMETRICAL KICK

The geometrical kick shot is very accurate. It is also an excellent method for figuring bank shots. To find the point of aim with this method, begin by drawing an imaginary vertical line from the cue ball to the rail. Place the tip of your cue stick at that point on the rail and lay the cue stick down pointing to the target pocket. (Be careful anytime you use your cue stick for measuring. You are not allowed to leave chalk marks or chalk cubes, etc. as reference markers on the rail. You could be called for a foul.) Now draw an imaginary line from the cue ball through the cue stick to the pocket directly opposite the target pocket. Finally, draw another imaginary line to the rail from the point at which the two diagonal lines intersect. This is your point of aim. Use center ball and a slow to medium speed (*Figure 29*).

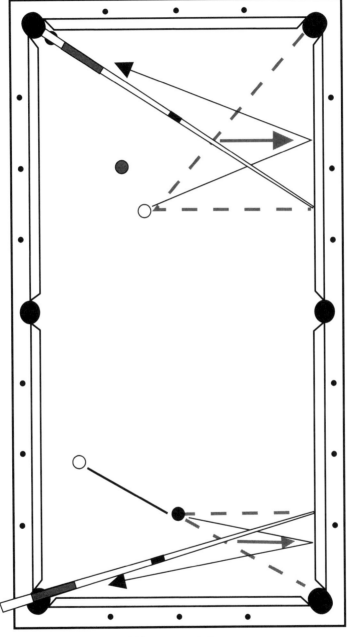

Figure 29

VANISHING POINT KICK

I first heard of this theory from a seasoned bar table player. I used the geometrical method for one-rail kicks and she used this vanishing point method. Once we discovered we were using different methods to make the same shots we suspended play for awhile and shared our knowledge of the two systems.

This method of kicking or banking shots is easy and quick to figure. With a little practice you can become very comfortable using it. It's based upon the vanishing point theory used in architectural drawings. Once you determine the vanishing point, it becomes your point of aim.

The vanishing point is determined simply by identifying the diamond (i.e., D2 or D4), on the opposite rail that is half the distance between the pocket to which you wish to bank and the pocket along the same rail that corresponds to the position of the ball. Extend an imaginary line from the appropriate pocket straight through the diamond and on to a spot about 5 feet away, generally a spot on another pool table or the wall. This is the vanishing point. Your reference point. Now draw an imaginary line from the cue ball (for a kick shot) or the object ball (for a bank) through the rail to the reference point. Your point of aim will be that point on the rail through which the line passes (*Figure 30*).

Depending upon the condition of the rails, the cloth and the actual distance to the available vanishing point, some adjustments might be necessary. I have found that in some situations I've had to determine the vanishing point on the rail through the extended diamond. In other situations I've had to determine the vanishing point along the outer edge of the diamond. If you play on the same table every day, you will quickly learn the points of aim.

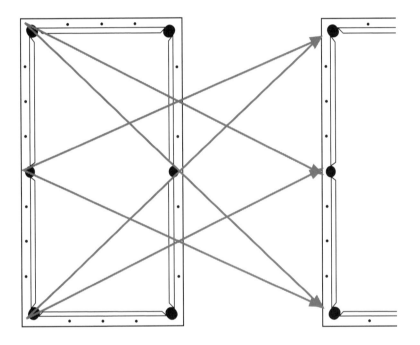

Figure 30

Use the same procedure to determine the vanishing point along the short rails. Extend the imaginary line from the corner pocket through the center diamond on the top rail to find the vanishing point.

Here is an example of the vanishing kick shot in action. I made this shot years ago in a small local 8-ball tournament. I had all but run out, missing a thin cut on the 8-ball into the side pocket. I watched it bounce around the jaws of the pocket before being spit out like a sour grape. It came to rest a few inches in front of the hole. My opponent made a couple of balls and missed his third shot, leaving me hooked on the 8-ball (*Figure 31*). Now, I had been practicing this vanishing point kick shot looking for an opportunity to use it. With a slow stroke to prevent following the 8-ball into the pocket, I won the game. Of course I have used it many times since, but that was the first.

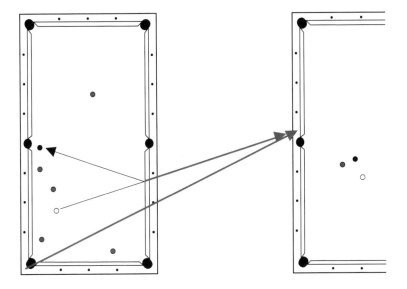

Figure 31

PARALLEL CUE BALL KICK

Here is another great method for figuring both kicks and bank shots. Find a spot on the table near the desired point of contact that is parallel to the cue ball. Place your cue tip on the rail halfway between the cue ball and the chosen spot. Lay your cue stick over the spot. Stroking center ball with a slow to medium speed, this is the path the ball will take. Now observe the distance from the path to the desired point of contact. Divide that distance in half to find the point of aim along the rail (*Figure 32*). This method is very accurate.

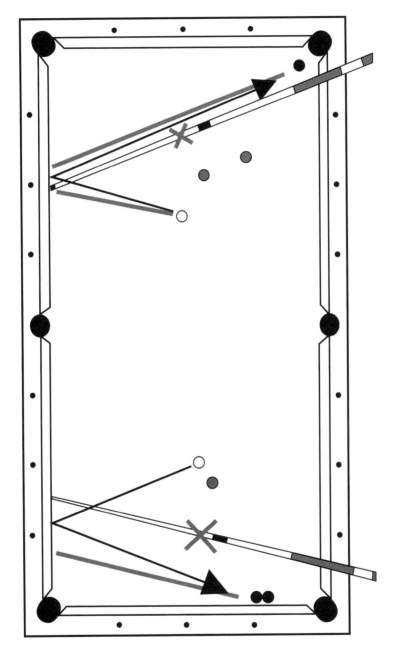

Figure 32

SHORT RAIL KICK

From the corner pocket, a medium stroke with no English aimed at the point on the short rail that extends out of the center diamond will go to the other corner pocket. Move the point of aim to the left half diamond and the ball will strike the sixth diamond on the long rail. Move the point of aim to the left another half diamond (now aimed to the extended first diamond on the short rail), and the ball goes to the side pocket. Move over yet another half diamond and the ball goes to the second diamond on the long rail. Likewise, if the cue ball is along any one of these paths going the other direction it will go to the corner pocket (*Figure 33*).

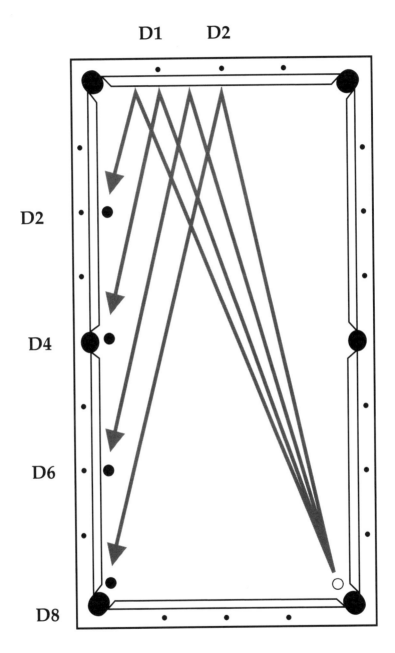

Figure 33

4 PLUS 4 KICK SHOT

As another memory tool, I call this shot the 4 plus 4 kick shot. As you will see, the diamonds that mark each path total the number four. Four plus four equals eight. Diamond eight just happens to be the number of the diamond in corner pocket.

For this shot number the diamonds on the short rail with D1 being the diamond furthest from the long rail you wish to kick. Each of these diamonds will correspond to the diamond along the long rail that brings the total count to four. There is a path between each set of corresponding diamonds that goes to the corner pocket. Make the shot with a slow to medium stroke using about one tip of inside English. Adjust for shots closer to the corner by aiming up to an inch or so further down the rail. For those shots that are beyond the path of diamond one along the foot rail to diamond three along the long rail, divide the distance in half to find the point of aim (*Figure 34*).

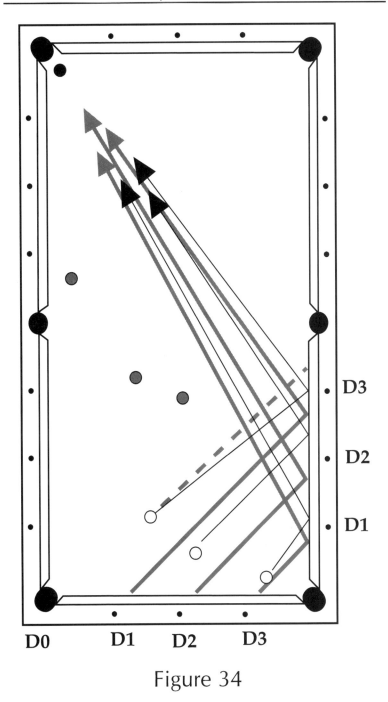

Figure 34

2 BY 4 KICK SHOT

    This shot is similar to the previous one. However, it is much more difficult to control. I seldom use it and was even hesitant to include it, but there are times when it will come in handy. I needed it badly not long ago in a local 8-ball tournament. I was hooked and could see no other way out. Although I did not pocket the object ball, I was able to kick it to a rail and avoid the ball-in-hand foul. Learn the shot even though it's tough.

    As another memory tool, I call this shot the 2 by 4 kick shot. The path for this shot is from the second diamond on the short rail to the fourth diamond on the long rail. Thus, 2 by 4 equals eight, once again, the corner pocket. Use about two tips of low, slightly outside English with a medium stroke. Coming out of the second diamond on the short rail aim just before the side pocket to kick to the corner pocket. Adjust in parallels. However, as with most of these shots, as the position of cue ball nears the side rail adjust the shot down rail a little to compensate (*Figure 35*).

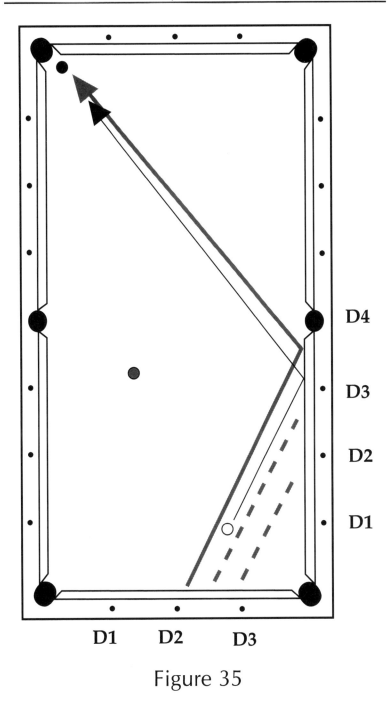

Figure 35

MIRROR KICK

This final kick shot is one of the best. It is used to kick balls that are as far as one diamond off the rail. It is also very accurate for actually pocketing balls that are within two or three inches of the rail. In fact, in order to get shape for the next shot, this is often the shot of choice, even though the object ball is not hooked.

The shot works as if you had a mirror along the rail. Simply measure the distance from the desired point of contact to the rail. Then, measure that distance from the rail straight outward toward the edge of the table. Using a slow-medium stroke, this is your point of aim (*Figure 36*). Of course, if you need to use English for one reason or another then the point of aim needs to be adjusted to compensate.

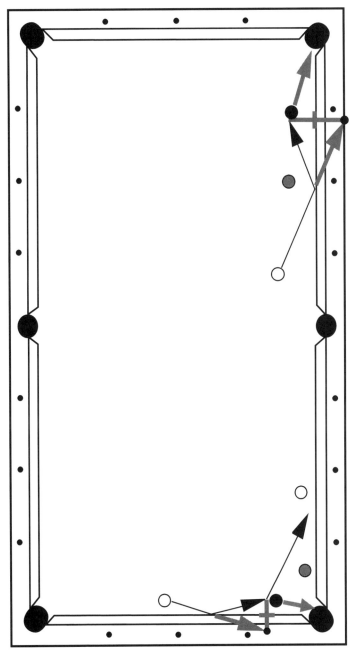

Figure 36

Glossary

Draw: A shot below center on the cue ball that generates backspin. This causes the cue ball to roll backward after contact with the object ball.

Extended diamond: That imaginary point on the rail that extends directly out of the diamond to the rail.

Extreme English: As far off center as possible without a miss cue.

First rail: The first rail the ball contacts as it travels around the table.

Follow: Over spin is applied to the cue ball either by ball speed or by striking it above center.

Foot rail: The short rail on any given shot that is nearest the cue ball.

Fourth rail: The fourth rail the ball contacts as it travels around the table.

Hooked: The cue ball is unable to make a direct hit on the object ball.

Inside English: This can be left or right English. It depends on the angle at which the ball contacts a rail or object ball. For our purposes, when a ball contacts a rail, spin is naturally transferred to the ball in the direction in which the ball is traveling. Inside English enhances that natural spin.

Head rail: The short rail on any given shot that is furthest from the cue ball.

Long rail: There are four rails, two of these are longer than the others and each is said to be a long rail.

O'clock: When describing English, it is common to refer to the point on the cue ball that the tip should contact as a number on a clock. As such, 3:00 is right English, center ball; 2:00 is right English, a little above center ball.

One tip English: The cue ball is struck off center by the width of one cue tip.

Outside English: This can left or right English. It depends on the angle at which the ball contacts a rail or object ball. For our purposes, when a ball contacts a rail, spin is naturally transferred to the ball in the direction in which the ball is traveling. Outside English impedes and even counteracts that natural spin.

Position of cue ball: Using the System, the cue ball anywhere in the path from a given position point to the corresponding diamond on the first rail is said to be in that given position.

Running English: Inside English.

Second rail: The second rail the ball contacts as it travels around the table.

Shape: Position for the next shot.

Short rail: There are four rails, two of these are shorter than the others and are each is said to be a short rail.

Tangent line: An imaginary line directly perpendicular to the point at which the two balls collide. Barring any draw or over spin on the cue ball, it will always travel along the tangent line after contacting the object ball.

Third rail: The third rail the ball contacts as it travels around the table.

Two tips English: The cue ball is struck off center by the width of two cue tips.